Fat Quarter Bags

LEISURE ARTS, INC. • Little Rock, Arkansas

EDITORIAL STAFF
Vice President of Editorial: Susan White Sullivan
Special Projects Director: Susan Frantz Wiles
Director of E-Commerce Services: Mark Hawkins
Creative Art Director: Katherine Laughlin
Technical Editor: Lisa Lancaster
Technical Writer: Frances Huddleston
Technical Associate: Jean Lewis
Art Category Manager: Lora Puls
Graphic Artist: Becca Snider Tally
Prepress Technician: Stephanie Johnson
Contributing Photographer: Mark Mathews
Contributing Photo Stylist: Christy Myers
Manager of E-Commerce: Robert Young

BUSINESS STAFF
President and Chief Executive Officer: Rick Barton
Vice President of Finance: Fred F. Pruss
Vice President of Sales-Retail Books: Martha Adams
Vice President of Mass Market: Bob Bewighouse
Vice President of Technology and Planning: Laticia Mull Dittrich
Director of Corporate Planning: Anne Martin
Information Technology Director: Brian Roden
Controller: Francis Caple
Senior Vice President of Operations: Jim Dittrich
Retail Customer Service Manager: Stan Raynor

Library of Congress Control Number: 2013933964

ISBN-13: 978-1-4647-0759-9

TABLE OF CONTENTS

Gather up your
FAT QUARTERS
and get ready for some fun!

Each of these eye-catching bags from Stephanie Prescott of A Quilter's Dream can be created with just six fat quarters. Study the photographed models to get a feel for how to mix and match fabrics for intriguing results. Most include color variations to demonstrate the dramatic power of fabric selection. Reflecting the scrappy nature of the designs, some bags have a different look on the front and back and all have roomy pockets inside. Cutting diagrams and rotary cutting tables are provided to help you get the most of each fat quarter. A fun way to play with pattern and color, these bags are truly a quilter's dream!

MEET THE DESIGNER

Stephanie Prescott of A Quilter's Dream specializes in designs that combine easy patterns with eclectic fabric collections. "I am addicted to the idea of what a fabric becomes when cut up in a quilt," she said.

Her passion for quilting grew out of helping at her mother's shop, A Quilter's Dream, in San Dimas, California. After several years of working together and branching out into kits, her mother moved to a resort area and Stephanie started running the shop.

Her first designs were used for giveaways and Block of the Months. "I officially began to design, package, and sell my patterns in 2007. A few years later, I closed the retail store and threw my efforts into pattern design, unusual and unexpected fabric selections for my kits, and trade shows." In 2012, Stephanie also partnered with E.E. Schenck on her first fabric line.

"One of the wonderful things I have discovered about quilting is that it grows with you," she said, "and your quilts reflect your changing esthetics, without you outgrowing it."

For more about Stephanie's work, visit AQuiltersDream.com or her company's Facebook page.

montecito

Finished Bag Size: 13½" x 11¾" x 4½" (34 cm x 30 cm x 11 cm)

SHOPPING LIST

Fat quarters are approximately 22" x 18" (56 cm x 46 cm).

☐ 6 assorted fat quarters (3 accent fabrics and 3 background fabrics)

☐ 1⅛ yds (1 m) of 45" (114 cm) wide Pellon® fusible fleece

Optional: For a more rigid bag bottom, you will also need the following to make bottom insert. (Bag shown does not have insert.)

☐ 1 piece of template plastic 13½" x 4½" (34 cm x 11 cm)

☐ 2 pieces of fabric 14⅛" x 5⅛" (36 cm x 13 cm) for **insert covers**

CUTTING THE PIECES

Follow tables and cutting diagrams and **Rotary Cutting**, *page 61, to cut fabric. All measurements include* ¼" *seam allowances.*

From *each* of fat quarters #1 and #2 (accent fabrics)

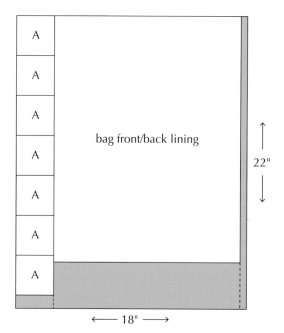

Piece	Cut	Size
square A	7	3" x 3"
bag front/back lining	1	18½" x 14½"

From fat quarter #3 (accent fabric)

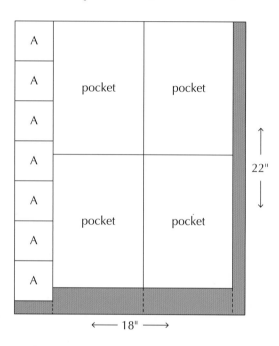

Piece	Cut	Size
square A	7	3" x 3"
pocket	4	10" x 7"

From fat quarter #4 (background fabric)

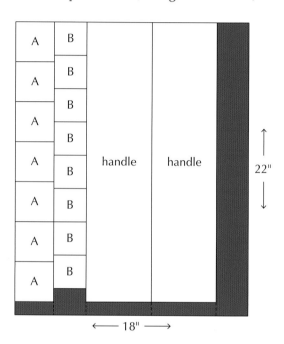

Piece	Cut	Size
square A	7	3" x 3"
square B	8	2½" x 2½"
handle	2	5" x 21"

From *each* of fat quarters #5 & #6 (background fabrics)

From fusible fleece

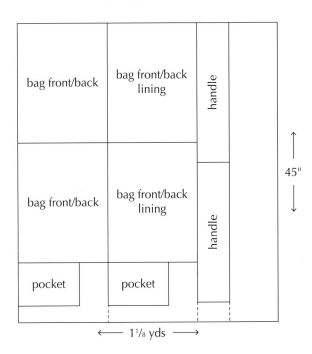

Piece	Cut	Size
square A	7	3" x 3"
square B	40	2½" x 2½"

Piece	Cut	Size
bag front/back and bag front/back lining	4	18" x 14"
pocket	2	9½" x 6½"
handle	2	5" x 21"

MAKING THE BAG FRONT AND BACK

*Follow **Piecing**, page 62, and **Pressing**, page 63, to make bag. Use ¹/₄" seam allowances throughout.*

Note: When fusing fleece to fabric, place fleece, fusible side up, on ironing board. Center fabric, right side up, on top of fleece. Iron on the fabric side; do not place hot iron directly on fusible fleece.

1. Draw a diagonal line on wrong side of each accent fabric **square A**.

2. With right sides together, place 1 accent fabric square A on top of 1 background fabric square A. Stitch ¹/₄" from each side of drawn line *(Fig. 1)*. Cut along drawn line and press seam allowances to darker fabric to make 2 **Triangle-Squares**. Trim Triangle-Squares to 2¹/₂" x 2¹/₂". Make 42 Triangle-Squares.

Fig. 1

Triangle-Square (make 42)

back

3. Referring to **Bag Front/Back** diagram, arrange 20 Triangle-Squares and 43 **squares B** into 7 Rows of 9 Triangle-Squares and squares B.

4. Sew Triangles-Squares and squares B into Rows. Sew Rows together to make **Bag Front**. Bag Front should measure 18¹/₂" x 14¹/₂".

5. Repeat Steps 3-4 to make **Bag Back**. *Note: You will have 2 Triangle-Squares and 2 squares B left over.*

Bag Front/Back

6. Fuse corresponding fleece pieces to Bag Front and Bag Back.

7. Follow **Quilting**, page 63, to quilt Bag Front and Bag Back as desired. Bag shown is machine quilted in the ditch around the accent fabric design.

MAKING THE BAG FRONT AND BACK LINING

1. Fuse corresponding fleece pieces to **bag front/back linings**.

2. Fuse corresponding fleece pieces to 2 **pockets**.

3. With right sides together and leaving one long edge open, sew 1 pocket with fleece and 1 pocket without fleece together. Clip corners, turn, and press. Repeat with remaining pockets.

4. With raw edges of pocket 2¹/₂" from bottom edge of lining, center 1 pocket horizontally on right side of bag front lining. Sew raw edge of pocket to bag front lining *(Fig. 2)*.

Fig. 2

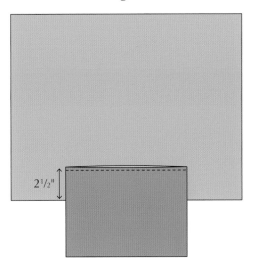

2¹/₂"

5. Press pocket up; pin. Topstitch ¹/₄" from side and bottom edges of pocket *(Fig. 3)*.

Fig. 3

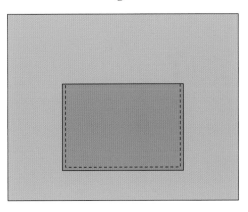

6. Repeat Steps 4-5 to sew pocket to bag back lining.

MAKING THE HANDLES

1. Fuse corresponding fleece pieces to **handles**.
2. Matching **wrong sides** and long edges, press 1 handle in half. Open up and press long edges to meet pressed crease **(Fig. 4)**. Matching folded edges, press handle in half again. Repeat with remaining handle.

Fig. 4

3. Topstitch approximately $^1/_8$" and $^3/_8$" from folded edges of each handle **(Fig. 5)**.

Fig. 5

4. Extending ends of handle $^1/_4$" beyond top of Bag Front, pin 1 handle to right side of Bag Front 4" from Bag Front sides **(Fig. 6)**. Keeping stitches within the $^1/_4$" seam allowance, zigzag stitch handle ends to Bag Front; stitch back and forth 2 or 3 times. Repeat to add remaining handle to Bag Back.

Fig. 6

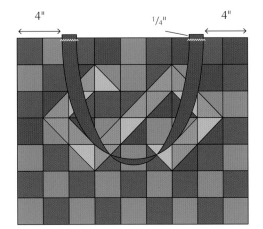

ASSEMBLING THE BAG

1. Sew Bag Front and Bag Back together along side and bottom edges to make **outer bag** **(Fig. 7)**. Do not turn outer bag right side out.

Fig. 7

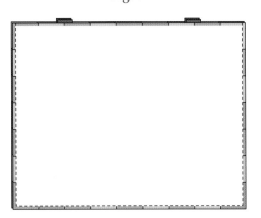

2. To form bottom corners of bag, match side and bottom seams **(Fig. 8)**. Sew across each corner $2^1/_4$" from corner point. Trim seam allowances to $^1/_4$". Turn outer bag right side out.

Fig. 8

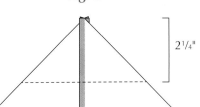

3. Leaving a 5" opening along bottom edge, repeat Steps 1-2 using lining pieces to make **bag lining**. Do not turn bag lining right side out.

4. Matching right sides and top edges, place outer bag inside bag lining. Sew outer bag and bag lining together along top edge. Turn bag right side out through opening in bag lining. Sew opening closed. Place bag lining inside outer bag.

5. Topstitch ¼" from top edge of bag.

6. To make optional **bottom insert**, sew **insert covers** together leaving 1 short end open. Clip corners and turn right side out. Slip template plastic in cover and stitch opening closed. Place bottom insert in bottom of bag.

This bright pink and turquoise Montecito bag measures 16" x 13" x 2" (41 cm x 33 cm x 5 cm). The bottom corners of the bag were made by sewing across the corners 1" from the corner points.

back

front

oceanside

Finished Bag Size: 14" x 12" x 3" (36 cm x 30 cm x 8 cm)

SHOPPING LIST

Fat quarters are approximately 22" x 18" (56 cm x 46 cm).

☐ 6 assorted fat quarters (2 accent fabrics and 4 background fabrics)

☐ 1 yd (91 cm) of 45" (114 cm) wide Pellon® fusible fleece

Optional: For a more rigid bag bottom, you will also need the following to make bottom insert. (Bag shown does not have insert.)

☐ 1 piece of template plastic 14" x 3" (36 cm x 8 cm)

☐ 2 pieces of fabric 14⅝" x 3⅝" (37 cm x 9 cm) for **insert covers**

CUTTING THE PIECES

*Follow tables and cutting diagrams and **Rotary Cutting**, page 61, to cut fabric. All measurements include ¹/₄" seam allowances.*

From fat quarter #1 (accent fabric)

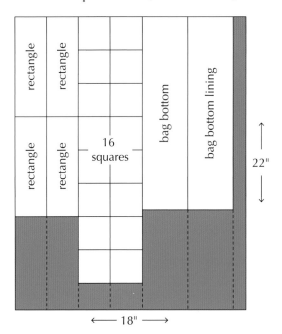

Piece	Cut	Size
rectangle	4	7¹/₂" x 2¹/₂"
square	16	2¹/₂" x 2¹/₂"
bag bottom and bag bottom lining	2	14¹/₂" x 3¹/₂"

From fat quarter #2 (accent fabric)

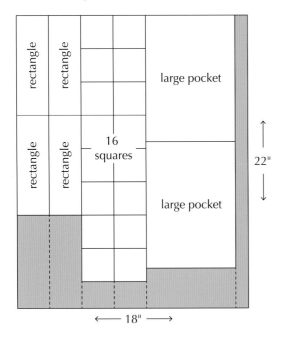

Piece	Cut	Size
rectangle	4	$7^1/_2$" x $2^1/_2$"
square	16	$2^1/_2$" x $2^1/_2$"
large pocket	2	$9^1/_2$" x 7"

From fat quarter #3 (background fabric)

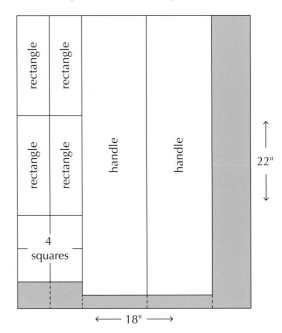

Piece	Cut	Size
rectangle	4	$7^1/_2$" x $2^1/_2$"
square	4	$2^1/_2$" x $2^1/_2$"
handle	2	5" x 21"

From *each* of fat quarters #4 and #5 (background fabrics)

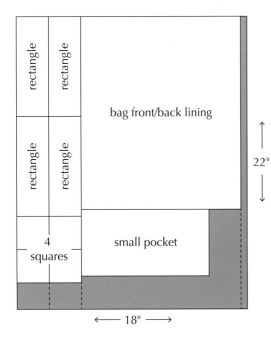

Piece	Cut	Size
rectangle	4	$7^1/_2$" x $2^1/_2$"
square	4	$2^1/_2$" x $2^1/_2$"
bag front/back lining	1	$14^1/_2$" x $12^1/_2$"
small pocket	1	10" x 5"

From fat quarter #6 (background fabric)

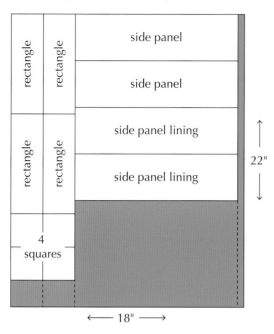

Piece	Cut	Size
rectangle	4	$7^1/_2$" x $2^1/_2$"
square	4	$2^1/_2$" x $2^1/_2$"
side panel and side panel lining	4	$3^1/_2$" x $12^1/_2$"

From fusible fleece

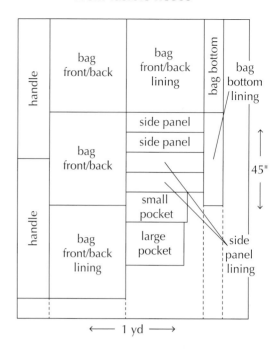

Piece	Cut	Size
handle	2	5" x 21"
bag front/back and bag front/back lining	4	14" x 12"
side panel and side panel lining	4	3" x 12"
small pocket	1	$9^1/_2$" x $4^1/_2$"
large pocket	1	9" x $6^1/_2$"
bag bottom and bag bottom lining	2	14" x 3"

back

MAKING THE BAG FRONT AND BACK

*Follow **Piecing**, page 62, and **Pressing**, page 63, to make bag. Use ¹⁄₄" seam allowances throughout.*

Note: When fusing fleece to fabric, place fleece, fusible side up, on ironing board. Center fabric, right side up, on top of fleece. Iron on the fabric side; do not place hot iron directly on fusible fleece.

1. Draw a diagonal line on wrong side of each **square**.
2. Select 2 **rectangles** and 8 **squares** from 1 accent fabric and 4 **rectangles** and 4 **squares** from 1 background fabric.
3. With right sides together, place 1 accent square on each end of 1 background rectangle and stitch along drawn lines *(Fig. 1)*. Trim ¹⁄₄" from stitching *(Fig. 2)* and press open to make **Unit 1**. Make 4 Unit 1's.

Fig. 1

Fig. 2

Unit 1 (make 4)

4. In the same manner, use background squares and accent rectangles to make 2 **Unit 2's**.

Unit 2 (make 2)

5. Sew 2 Unit 1's and 1 Unit 2 together to make **Unit 3**. Unit 3 should measure 7¹⁄₂" x 6¹⁄₂" including seam allowances. Make 2 Unit 3's.

Unit 3 (make 2)

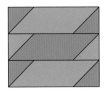

6. Select the remaining 2 rectangles and 8 squares from same accent fabric as used in Unit 3 and 4 rectangles and 4 squares from a different background fabric.

7. With right sides together, place 1 accent square on each end of 1 background rectangle and stitch along drawn lines *(Fig. 3)*. Trim ¼" from stitching *(Fig. 4)* and press open to make **Unit 4**. Make 4 Unit 4's.

Fig. 3

Fig. 4

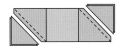

Unit 4 (make 4)

8. In the same manner, use background squares and accent rectangles to make 2 **Unit 5's**.

Unit 5 (make 2)

9. Sew 2 Unit 4's and 1 Unit 5 together to make **Unit 6**. Unit 6 should measure 7½" x 6½" including seam allowances. Make 2 Unit 6's.

Unit 6 (make 2)

10. Sew 2 Unit 3's and 2 Unit 6's together to make **Bag Front**. Bag Front should measure 14½" x 12½" including seam allowances.

Bag Front

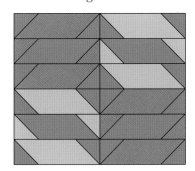

11. Using remaining rectangles and squares, follow Steps 2-10 to make **Bag Back**.

Bag Back

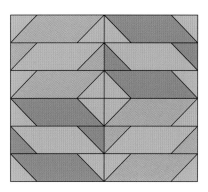

12. Fuse corresponding fleece pieces to Bag Front and Bag Back.
13. Follow **Quilting**, page 63, to quilt Bag Front and Bag Back if desired. Bag shown is not quilted.

MAKING THE BAG FRONT AND BACK LINING

1. Fuse corresponding fleece pieces to **bag front/back linings**.
2. Fuse corresponding fleece pieces to 1 **large pocket** and 1 **small pocket**.
3. With right sides together and leaving one long edge open, sew 2 large pockets together. Clip corners, turn, and press. Repeat with small pockets.
4. With raw edges of pocket 2" from bottom edge of lining, center large pocket horizontally on right side of bag front lining. Sew raw edge of pocket to bag front lining *(Fig. 5)*.

Fig. 5

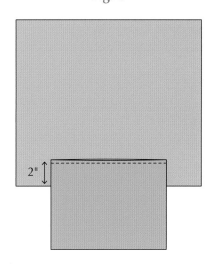

17

5. Press pocket up; pin. Topstitch $1/4$" from side and bottom edges of pocket (*Fig. 6*).

Fig. 6

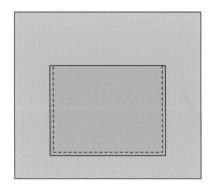

6. With raw edges of pocket 3" from bottom edge of lining, repeat Steps 4-5 to sew small pocket to bag back lining.

MAKING THE BAG BOTTOM AND SIDE PANELS

1. Fuse corresponding fleece pieces to **bag bottom** and **bag bottom linings**.
2. Fuse corresponding fleece pieces to **side panels** and **side panel linings**.

MAKING THE HANDLES

1. Fuse corresponding fleece pieces to **handles**.
2. Matching *wrong sides* and long edges, press 1 handle in half. Open up and press long edges to meet pressed crease (*Fig. 7*). Matching folded edges, press handle in half again. Repeat with remaining handle.

Fig. 7

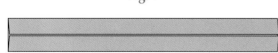

3. Topstitch approximately $1/8$" from folded edges and in the center of each handle (*Fig. 8*).

Fig. 8

4. Extending ends of handle $1/4$" beyond top of Bag Front, pin 1 handle to right side of Bag Front $3 1/4$" from Bag Front sides (*Fig. 9*). Keeping stitches within the $1/4$" seam allowance, zigzag stitch handle ends to Bag Front; stitch back and forth 2 or 3 times. Repeat to add remaining handle to Bag Back.

Fig. 9

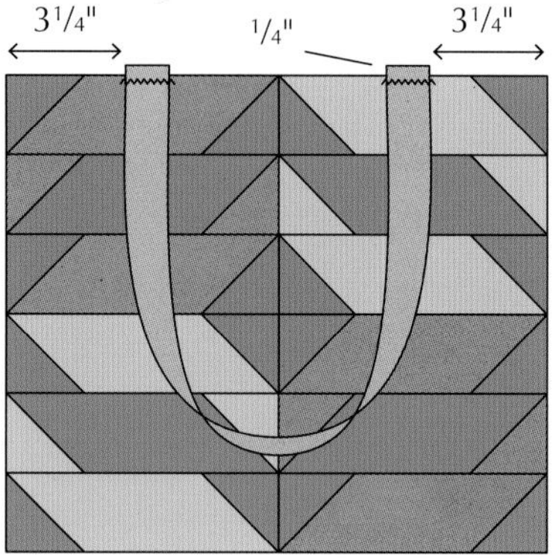

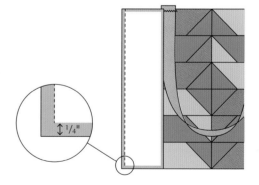

ASSEMBLING THE BAG

1. Aligning top edges and stopping and backstitching $1/4$" from bottom edge of side panel, sew 1 side panel to one side of Bag Front (*Fig. 10*). Sew remaining side panel to other side of Bag Front (*Fig. 11*).

Fig. 10

Fig. 11

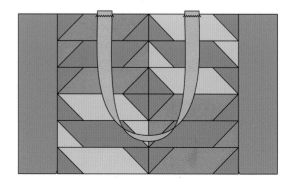

2. Starting and stopping ¹/₄" from short edges of bag bottom and backstitching at beginning and end, sew bag bottom to bottom edge of Bag Front *(Fig. 12)*.

Fig. 12

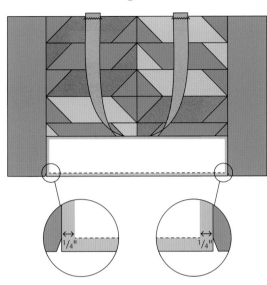

3. In the same manner, sew bag bottom to bottom edge of Bag Back.
4. Stopping and backstitching ¹/₄" from bottom corners, sew side panels to bag back *(Fig. 13)*. Starting and stopping ¹/₄" from corners and backstitching at beginning and end, sew bottom edges of side panels to short edges of bag bottom to make **outer bag**. Turn outer bag right side out.

Fig. 13

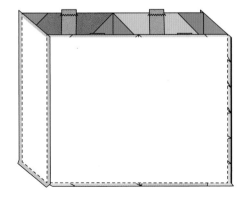

5. Leaving a 5" opening along one bottom edge, repeat Steps 1-4 using lining pieces to make **bag lining**. Do not turn bag lining right side out.
6. Matching right sides and top edges, place outer bag inside bag lining. Sew outer bag and bag lining together along top edge. Turn bag right side out through opening in bag lining. Sew opening closed. Place bag lining inside outer bag.

7. Topstitch ¹/₄" from top edge of bag.
8. To make optional **bottom insert**, sew **insert covers** together leaving 1 short end open. Clip corners and turn right side out. Slip template plastic in cover and stitch opening closed. Place bottom insert in bottom of bag.

front

back

This version of Oceanside was made with 4 orange/gold print fat quarters and 2 black print fat quarters. The high contrast of the prints results in a bold design.

pismo beach

Finished Bag Size: 12" x 12" x 3" (30 cm x 30 cm x 8 cm)

SHOPPING LIST

Fat quarters are approximately 22" x 18" (56 cm x 46 cm).

☐ 6 assorted fat quarters (2 accent fabrics for "trellis" and 4 background fabrics)

☐ 1 yd (91 cm) of 45" (114 cm) wide Pellon® fusible fleece

Optional: *For a more rigid bag bottom, you will also need the following to make bottom insert. (Bag shown does not have insert.)*

☐ 1 piece of template plastic 12" x 3" (30 cm x 8 cm)

☐ 2 pieces of fabric 12⅝" x 3⅝" (32 cm x 9 cm) for **insert covers**

CUTTING THE PIECES

*Follow tables and cutting diagrams and **Rotary Cutting**, page 61, to cut fabric. All measurements include ¹/₄" seam allowances.*

From *each* of fat quarters #1 and #2 (accent fabrics)

Piece	Cut	Size
square A	20	3¹/₂" x 3¹/₂"
bag bottom and bag bottom lining	1	15¹/₂" x 3¹/₂"

From *each* of fat quarters #3 and #4 (background fabrics)

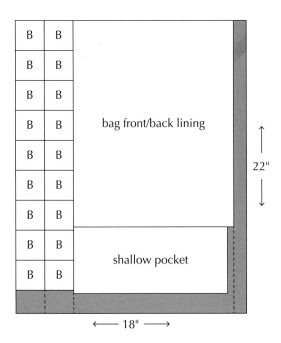

Piece	Cut	Size
square B	18	$2^{1}/_{4}"$ x $2^{1}/_{4}"$
bag front/back lining	1	$15^{1}/_{2}"$ x $12^{1}/_{2}"$
shallow pocket	1	$12"$ x $5"$

From fat quarter #5 (background fabric)

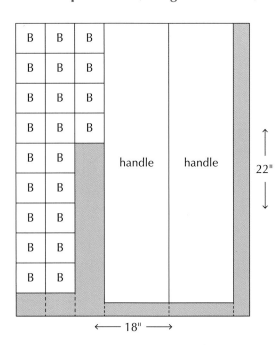

Piece	Cut	Size
square B	22	$2^{1}/_{4}"$ x $2^{1}/_{4}"$
handle	2	$5"$ x $21"$

From fat quarter #6 (background fabric)

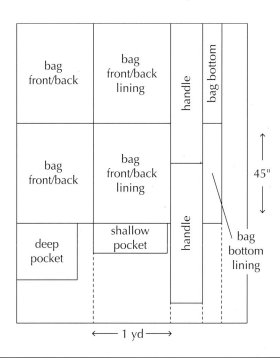

Piece	Cut	Size
square B	22	$2^1/_4"$ x $2^1/_4"$
deep pocket	2	10" x 9"

From fusible fleece

Piece	Cut	Size
bag front/back and bag front/back lining	4	15" x 12"
deep pocket	1	$9^1/_2"$ x $8^1/_2"$
shallow pocket	1	$11^1/_2"$ x $4^1/_2"$
handle	2	5" x 21"
bag bottom and bag bottom lining	2	15" x 3"

MAKING THE BAG FRONT AND BACK

*Follow **Piecing**, page 62, and **Pressing**, page 63, to make bag. Use ¹/₄" seam allowances throughout.*

Note: When fusing fleece to fabric, place fleece, fusible side up, on ironing board. Center fabric, right side up, on top of fleece. Iron on the fabric side; do not place hot iron directly on fusible fleece.

1. Draw a diagonal line on wrong side of each **square B**.
2. For Unit, select 1 **square A** and 2 matching squares B.

3. With right sides together, place 1 square B on 1 corner of square A and stitch along drawn line (**Fig. 1**). Trim ¹/₄" from stitching (**Fig. 2**) and press open (**Fig. 3**).

Fig. 1

Fig. 2

Fig. 3

back

4. In the same manner, sew remaining square B to opposite corner of square A to make **Unit**.
5. Repeat Steps 2-4 to make 40 Units.

Unit (make 40)

6. Referring to **Bag Front** diagram, arrange 20 Units with the same accent fabric into 4 Rows of 5 Units.
7. Sew Units together into Rows. Sew Rows together to make Bag Front. Bag Front should measure 15½" x 12½" including seam allowances.
8. Repeat Steps 6-7 make **Bag Back**. Bag Back should measure 15½" x 12½" including seam allowances.

Bag Front/Back

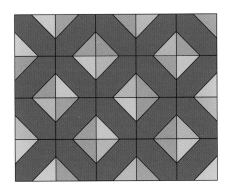

9. Fuse corresponding fleece pieces to Bag Front and Bag Back.
10. Follow **Quilting**, page 63, to quilt Bag Front and Bag Back as desired. Bag shown has a single line quilted through the center of the "trellis."

MAKING THE BAG FRONT AND BACK LINING

1. Fuse corresponding fleece pieces to **bag front/back linings**.
2. Fuse corresponding fleece pieces to 1 **deep pocket** and 1 **shallow pocket**.
3. With right sides together and leaving one long edge open, sew 2 shallow pockets together. Clip corners, turn, and press. Repeat with deep pockets.

4. With raw edges of pocket 3" from bottom edge of lining, center shallow pocket horizontally on right side of bag front lining. Sew raw edge of pocket to bag front lining *(Fig. 4)*.

Fig. 4

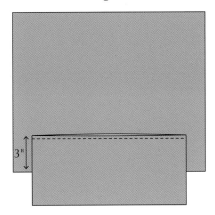

5. Press pocket up; pin. Topstitch ¼" from side and bottom edges of pocket. Topstitch a vertical divider line in center of pocket *(Fig. 5)*.

Fig. 5

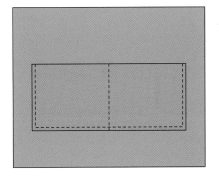

6. With raw edges of pocket 2½" from bottom edge of lining and omitting the vertical divider line, repeat Steps 4-5 to sew deep pocket to bag back lining.

MAKING THE BAG BOTTOM

1. Fuse corresponding fleece pieces to **bag bottom** and **bag bottom lining**.

MAKING THE HANDLES

1. Fuse corresponding fleece pieces to **handles**.
2. Matching **wrong sides** and long edges, press 1 handle in half. Open up and press long edges to meet pressed crease *(Fig. 6)*. Matching folded edges, press handle in half again. Repeat with remaining handle.

Fig. 6

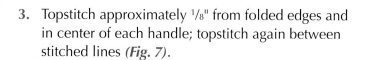

3. Topstitch approximately ⅛" from folded edges and in center of each handle; topstitch again between stitched lines *(Fig. 7)*.

Fig. 7

4. Extending ends of handle ¼" beyond top of Bag Front, pin 1 handle to right side of Bag Front 3¼" from Bag Front sides *(Fig. 8)*. Keeping stitches within the ¼" seam allowance of the Bag Front, zigzag stitch handle ends to Bag Front; stitch back and forth 2 or 3 times. Repeat to add remaining handle to Bag Back.

Fig. 8

3¼" ¼" 3¼"

ASSEMBLING THE BAG

1. Sew Bag Front, bag bottom, and Bag Back together *(Fig. 9)*.

Fig. 9

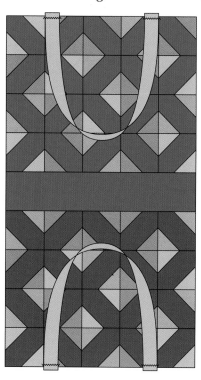

2. Matching right sides and top edges, fold bag in half and stitch side edges to make **outer bag** *(Fig. 10)*. Do not turn outer bag right side out.

Fig. 10

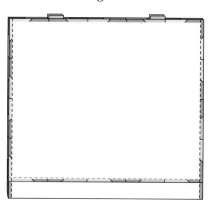

3. To form each bottom corner of bag, align 1 side seam to center of bag bottom. Sew across bag bottom 1½" from corner point *(Fig. 11)*. Trim seam allowances to ¼". Turn outer bag right side out.

Fig. 11

4. Leaving a 5" opening along one bottom edge, repeat Steps 1-3 using lining pieces to make **bag lining**. Do not turn bag lining right side out.

5. Matching right sides and top edges, place outer bag inside bag lining. Sew outer bag and bag lining together along top edge. Turn bag right side out through opening in bag lining. Sew opening closed. Place bag lining inside outer bag.

6. Topstitch ¼" from top edge of bag.

7. To make optional **bottom insert**, sew **insert covers** together leaving 1 short end open. Clip corners and turn right side out. Slip template plastic in cover and stitch opening closed. Place bottom insert in bottom of bag.

front

back

Aquas, greens, and yellows were used to create this vibrant version of Pismo Beach.

san clemente

Finished Bag Size: 17½" x 11½" x 3" (44 cm x 29 cm x 8 cm)

CUTTING THE PIECES

*Follow tables and cutting diagrams and **Rotary Cutting**, page 61, to cut fabric. All measurements include ¼" seam allowances.*

From fat quarter #1

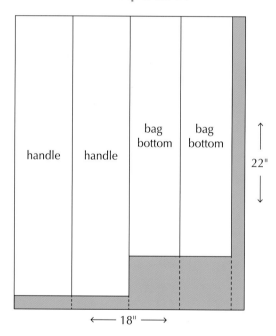

Piece	Cut	Size
handle	2	4½" x 21"
bag bottom	2	18" x 4"

From *each* of fat quarters #2 and #3

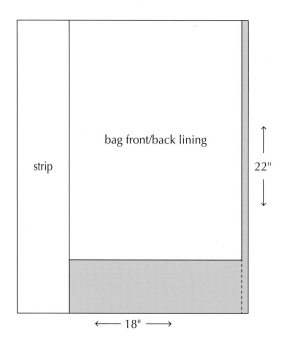

Piece	Cut	Size
strip	1	4" wide
bag front/back lining	1	18" x 13½"

From *each* of fat quarters #4 and #5

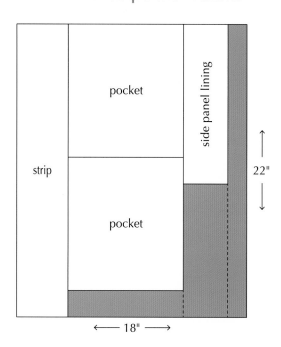

Piece	Cut	Size
strip	1	4" wide
pocket	2	10" x 9"
side panel lining	1	3½" x 12"

From fat quarter #6

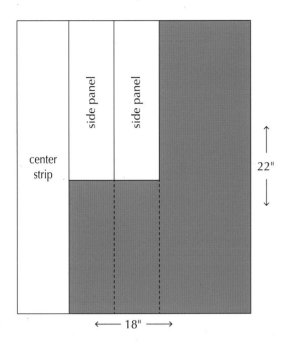

Piece	Cut	Size
center strip	1	4" wide
side panel	2	3¹/₂" x 12"

From fusible fleece

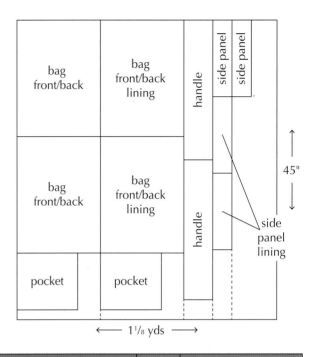

Piece	Cut	Size
bag front/back and bag front/back lining	4	17¹/₂" x 13"
pocket	2	9¹/₂" x 8¹/₂"
handle	2	4¹/₂" x 21"
side panel and side panel lining	4	3" x 11¹/₂"

MAKING THE BAG FRONT AND BACK

Follow Piecing, page 62, and Pressing, page 63, to make bag. Use ¹/₄" seam allowances throughout.

Note: When fusing fleece to fabric, place fleece, fusible side up, on ironing board. Center fabric, right side up, on top of fleece. Iron on the fabric side; do not place hot iron directly on fusible fleece.

1. With **center strip** in center, sew center strip and 4 **strips** together to make **Strip Set**. Cut across Strip Set at 10" intervals to make 2 **Units**.

Strip Set

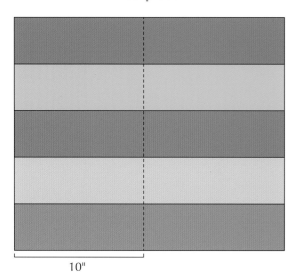

10"

Unit (make 2)

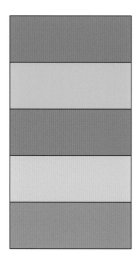

2. Sew 1 **bag bottom** and 1 Unit together to make **Bag Front**. Bag Front should measure 18" x 13¹/₂" including seam allowances. Repeat to make **Bag Back**.

Bag Front/Back (make 2)

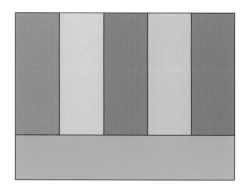

3. Fuse corresponding fleece pieces to Bag Front and Bag Back.
4. Follow **Quilting**, page 63, to quilt Bag Front and Bag Back as desired. Bag shown is quilted in the ditch.

MAKING THE BAG FRONT AND BACK LINING

1. Fuse corresponding fleece pieces to **bag front/back linings**.
2. Fuse corresponding fleece pieces to 2 **pockets** of different fabrics.
3. With right sides together and leaving one long edge open, sew 2 matching pockets together. Clip corners, turn, and press. Repeat with remaining pockets.

4. With raw edges of pocket 2" from bottom edge of lining, center 1 pocket horizontally on right side of bag front lining. Sew raw edge of pocket to bag front lining *(Fig. 1)*.

Fig. 1

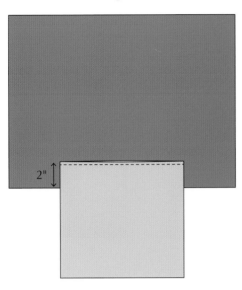

5. Press pocket up; pin. Topstitch ¹⁄₄" from side and bottom edges of pocket *(Fig. 2)*.

Fig. 2

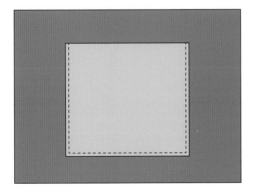

6. Repeat Steps 4-5 to sew pocket to bag back lining.

MAKING THE SIDE PANELS

1. Fuse corresponding fleece pieces to **side panels** and **side panel linings**.

MAKING THE HANDLES

1. Fuse corresponding fleece pieces to **handles**.
2. Matching ***wrong sides*** and long edges, press 1 handle in half. Open up and press long edges to meet pressed crease *(Fig. 3)*. Matching folded edges, press handle in half again. Repeat with remaining handle.

Fig. 3

3. Topstitch approximately ¹⁄₈" from folded edges and in center of each handle *(Fig. 4)*.

Fig. 4

4. Extending ends of handle ¼" beyond top of Bag Front, pin 1 handle to right side of Bag Front 4¾" from Bag Front sides *(Fig. 5)*. Keeping stitches within the ¼" seam allowance, zigzag stitch handle ends to Bag Front; stitch back and forth 2 or 3 times. Repeat to add remaining handle to Bag Back.

2. Aligning top edges and stopping and backstitching ¼" from bottom edge of side panel, sew 1 side panel to one side of Bag Front *(Fig. 7)*. Sew remaining side panel to other side of Bag Front *(Fig. 8)*.

Fig. 7

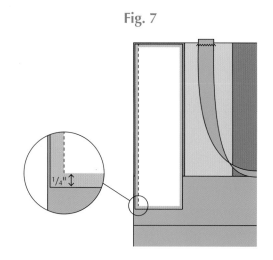

Fig. 5

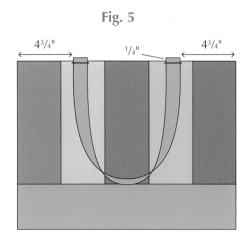

ASSEMBLING THE BAG

1. Sew Bag Front and Bag Back together along bottom edge *(Fig. 6)*.

Fig. 8

Fig. 6

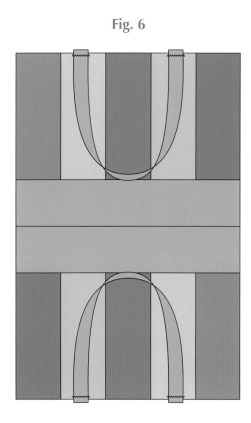

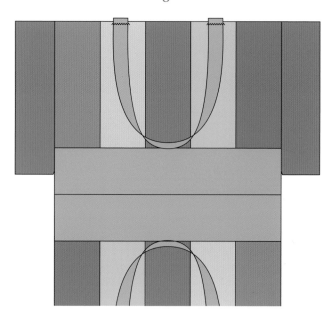

3. In the same manner, sew side panels to sides of Bag Back *(Fig. 9)*.

Fig. 9

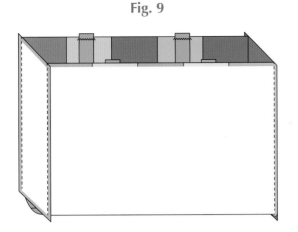

4. Backstitching at beginning and end of stitching, sew bottom edges of side panels to Bag Front/Back *(Fig. 10)* to complete **outer bag**. Turn outer bag right side out.

Fig. 10

5. Leaving a 5" opening along bottom edge, repeat Steps 1-4 using lining pieces to make **bag lining**. Do not turn bag lining right side out.

6. Matching right sides and top edges, place outer bag inside bag lining. Sew outer bag and bag lining together along top edge. Turn bag right side out through opening in bag lining. Sew opening closed. Place bag lining inside outer bag.

7. Topstitch ¹/₄" from top edge of bag.

8. To make optional **bottom insert**, sew **insert covers** together leaving 1 short end open. Clip corners and turn right side out. Slip template plastic in cover and stitch opening closed. Place bottom insert in bottom of bag.

This San Clemente bag was made using 1 black tone-on-tone, 3 black print, and 2 cream print fat quarters.

santa barbara

Finished Bag Size: 14" x 11½" x 3" (36 cm x 29 cm x 8 cm)

CUTTING THE PIECES

*Follow tables and cutting diagrams and **Rotary Cutting**, page 61, to cut fabric. All measurements include ¼" seam allowances.*

From *each* of fat quarters #1 and #2 (accent fabrics)

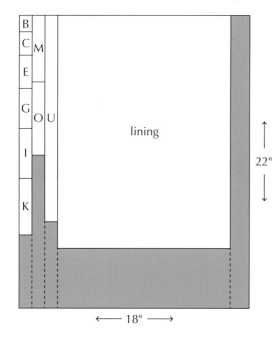

Piece	Cut	Size
rectangle B	1	1" x 1¼"
rectangle C	1	1" x 1¾"
rectangle E	1	1" x 2½"
rectangle G	1	1" x 3"
rectangle I	1	1" x 3¾"
rectangle K	1	1" x 4¼"
rectangle M	1	1" x 5"
rectangle O	1	1" x 5½"
rectangle U	1	1" x 15½"
bag front/back lining	1	17½" x 13½"

From *each* of fat quarters #3 and #4 (accent fabrics)

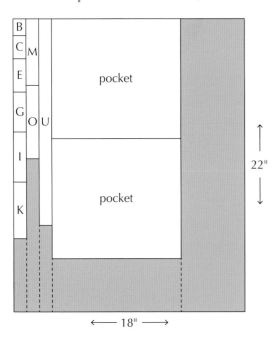

Piece	Cut	Size
rectangle B	1	1" x 1¼"
rectangle C	1	1" x 1¾"
rectangle E	1	1" x 2½"
rectangle G	1	1" x 3"
rectangle I	1	1" x 3¾"
rectangle K	1	1" x 4¼"
rectangle M	1	1" x 5"
rectangle O	1	1" x 5½"
rectangle U	1	1" x 15½"
pocket	2	10" x 9"

From *each* of fat quarters #5 and #6 (background fabric)

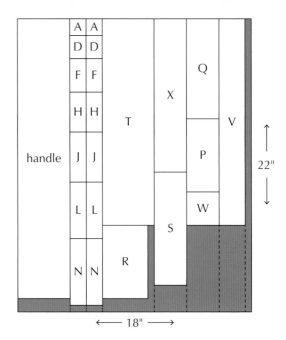

Piece	Cut	Size
handle	1	4" x 21"
square A	2	1¼" x 1¼"
rectangle D	2	1¼" x 1¾"
rectangle F	2	1¼" x 2½"
rectangle H	2	1¼" x 3"
rectangle J	2	1¼" x 3¾"
rectangle L	2	1¼" x 4¼"
rectangle N	2	1¼" x 5"
rectangle P	1	2½" x 5½"
rectangle Q	1	2½" x 7½"
rectangle R	1	3½" x 5½"
rectangle S	1	2½" x 8½"
rectangle T	1	4" x 15½"
rectangle V	1	2" x 15½"
square W	1	2½" x 2½"
rectangle X	1	2½" x 11½"

From fusible fleece

bag front/back	bag front/back lining	handle	
bag front/back	bag front/back lining	handle	
pocket	pocket		

45"

← 1 yd →

Piece	Cut	Size
bag front/back and back/front lining	4	17" x 13"
pocket	2	9$\frac{1}{2}$" x 8$\frac{1}{2}$"
handle	2	4" x 21"

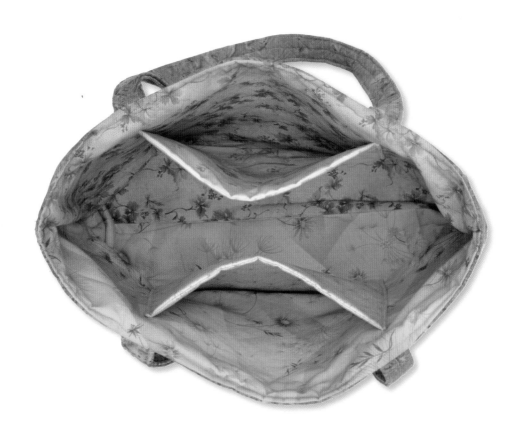

MAKING THE BAG FRONT AND BACK

*Follow **Piecing**, page 62, and **Pressing**, page 63, to make bag. Use ¹/₄" seam allowances throughout.*

Note: When fusing fleece to fabric, place fleece, fusible side up, on ironing board. Center fabric, right side up, on top of fleece. Iron on the fabric side; do not place hot iron directly on fusible fleece.

1. For **Swirl Block**, select pieces **A, D, F, H, J, L,** and **N** from 1 background fabric and pieces **B, C, E, G, I, K, M,** and **O** from 1 accent fabric.
2. Sew **square A** and **rectangle B** together to make **Unit 1**.

Unit 1

3. Sew **rectangle C, rectangle D,** and Unit 1 together to make **Unit 2**.

Unit 2

4. Continuing in alphabetical order, add **rectangles E-O** to make **Swirl Block**. Block should measure 5¹/₂" x 5¹/₂" including seam allowances.
5. Repeat Steps 1-4 to make a total of 4 Swirl Blocks.

Swirl Block (make 4)

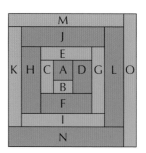

6. For **Bag Front**, select 2 Swirl Blocks and 1 each of **pieces P-T** and **V-X** from the same background fabric. Select 1 **rectangle U** from each of the same accent fabrics in the Blocks.
7. Sew 1 Block, **rectangle P**, and then **rectangle Q** together to make **Unit 3**. Unit 3 should measure 7¹/₂" x 7¹/₂" including seam allowances.

Unit 3

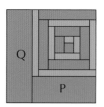

8. Sew 1 Block, **rectangle R**, and then **rectangle S** together to make **Unit 4**. Unit 4 should measure 8¹/₂" x 7¹/₂" including seam allowances.

Unit 4

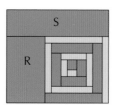

9. Sew **rectangle T** and 1 **rectangle U** from same accent fabric as in Unit 4 together to make **Unit 5**.

Unit 5

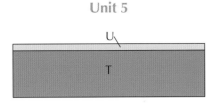

10. Sew **rectangle V** and 1 **rectangle U** from same accent fabric as in Unit 3, and then **square W** together to make **Unit 6**.

Unit 6

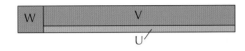

11. Referring to **Assembly Diagram**, sew Unit 3, Unit 4, Unit 5, **rectangle X**, and Unit 6 together to make **Bag Front**. Bag Front should measure 17¹/₂" x 13¹/₂" including seam allowances.

Assembly Diagram

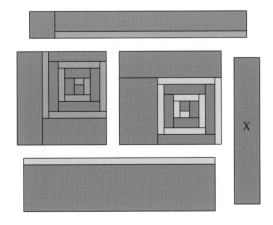

12. Using remaining pieces, repeat Steps 6-11 to make **Bag Back**. Bag Back should measure 17¹/₂" x 13¹/₂" including seam allowances.

Bag Front/Back

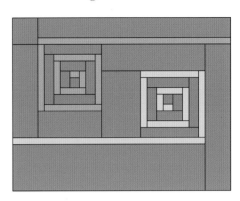

13. Fuse corresponding fleece pieces to Bag Front and Bag Back.
14. Follow **Quilting**, page 63, to quilt Bag Front and Bag Back as desired. Bag shown is machine outline quilted around the swirls.

MAKING THE BAG FRONT AND BACK LINING

1. Fuse corresponding fleece pieces to **bag front/back linings**.
2. Fuse corresponding fleece pieces to 2 **pockets** of different fabrics.
3. With right sides together and leaving one long edge open, sew 2 matching pockets together. Clip corners, turn, and press. Repeat with remaining pockets.

4. With raw edges of pocket 3" from bottom edge of lining, center 1 pocket horizontally on right side of bag front lining. Sew raw edge of pocket to bag front lining *(Fig. 1)*.

Fig. 1

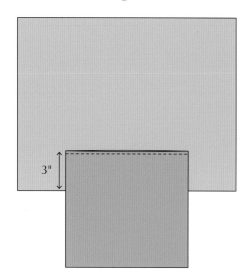

3"

5. Press pocket up; pin. Topstitch ¹/₄" from side and bottom edges of pocket *(Fig. 2)*.

Fig. 2

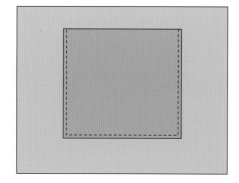

6. Repeat Steps 4-5 to sew pocket to bag back lining.

MAKING THE HANDLES

1. Fuse corresponding fleece pieces to **handles**.
2. Matching *wrong sides* and long edges, press 1 handle in half. Open up and press long edges to meet pressed crease *(Fig. 3)*. Matching folded edges, press handle in half again. Repeat with remaining handle.

Fig. 3

3. Topstitch approximately ¹/₈" from folded edges and in center of each handle *(Fig. 4)*.

Fig. 4

4. Extending ends of handle ¹/₄" beyond top of Bag Front, pin 1 handle to right side of Bag Front 4¹/₄" from Bag Front sides *(Fig. 5)*. Keeping stitches within the ¹/₄" seam allowance, zigzag stitch handle ends to Bag Front; stitch back and forth 2 or 3 times. Repeat to add remaining handle to Bag Back.

Fig. 5

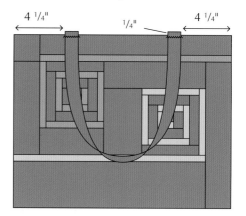

4 ¹/₄"　　¹/₄"　　4 ¹/₄"

ASSEMBLING THE BAG

1. Sew Bag Front and Bag Back together along side and bottom edges to make **outer bag** *(Fig. 6)*. Do not turn outer bag right side out.

Fig. 6

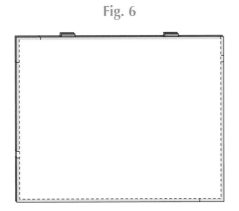

2. To form bottom corners of bag, match side and bottom seams *(Fig. 7)*. Sew across each corner 1¹/₂" from corner point. Trim seam allowances to ¹/₄". Turn outer bag right side out.

Fig. 7

1¹/₂"

3. Leaving a 5" opening along bottom edge, repeat Steps 1-2 using lining pieces to make **bag lining**. Do not turn bag lining right side out.

4. Matching right sides and top edges, place outer bag inside bag lining. Sew outer bag and bag lining together along top edge. Turn bag right side out through opening in bag lining. Sew opening closed. Place bag lining inside outer bag.

5. Topstitch ¹/₄" from top edge of bag.

6. To make optional **bottom insert**, sew **insert covers** together leaving 1 short end open. Clip corners and turn right side out. Slip template plastic in cover and stitch opening closed. Place bottom insert in bottom of bag.

back

sausalito

Finished Bag Size: 16" x 11½" x 3" (41 cm x 29 cm x 8 cm)

Shopping List

Fat quarters are approximately 22" x 18" (56 cm x 46 cm).
- ☐ 6 assorted fat quarters
- ☐ 1⅛ yd (1 m) of 45" (114 cm) wide Pellon® fusible fleece

Optional: For a more rigid bag bottom, you will also need the following to make bottom insert. (Bag shown does not have insert.)
- ☐ 1 piece of template plastic 16" x 3" (41 cm x 8 cm)
- ☐ 2 pieces of fabric 16⅝" x 3⅝" (42 cm x 9 cm) for **insert covers**

CUTTING THE PIECES

*Follow tables and cutting diagrams and **Rotary Cutting**, page 61, to cut fabric. All measurements include ¼" seam allowances.*

From fat quarter #1

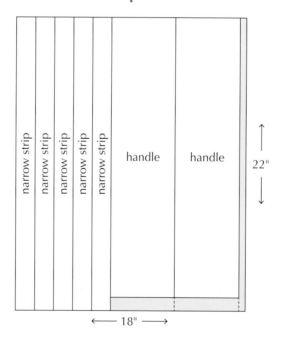

Piece	Cut	Size
narrow strip	5	1½" wide
handle	2	5" x 21"

From fat quarter #2

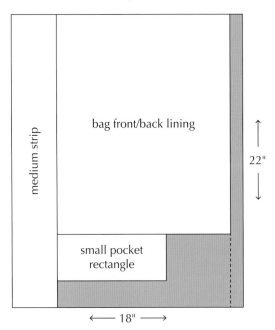

Piece	Cut	Size
medium strip	1	$3^{1}/_{2}$" wide
bag front/back lining	1	$16^{1}/_{2}$" x $13^{1}/_{2}$"
small pocket rectangle	1	$8^{1}/_{2}$" x $3^{1}/_{2}$"

From fat quarter #3

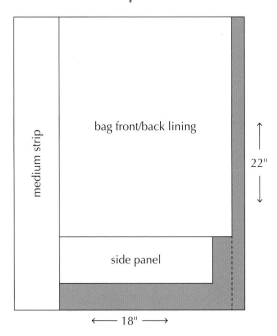

Piece	Cut	Size
medium strip	1	$3^{1}/_{2}$" wide
bag front/back lining	1	$16^{1}/_{2}$" x $13^{1}/_{2}$"
side panel	1	$3^{1}/_{2}$" x 12"

From fat quarter #4

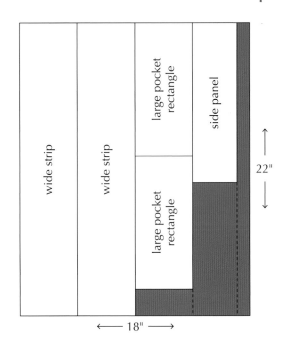

Piece	Cut	Size
wide strip	2	$4^{1}/_{2}$" wide
large pocket rectangle	2	10" x $4^{1}/_{2}$"
side panel	1	$3^{1}/_{2}$" x 12"

From fat quarter #5

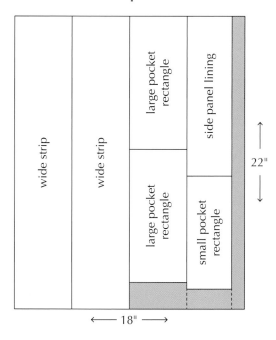

Piece	Cut	Size
wide strip	2	$4^1/_2$" wide
large pocket rectangle	2	10" x $4^1/_2$"
side panel lining	1	$3^1/_2$" x 12"
small pocket rectangle	1	$8^1/_2$" x $3^1/_2$"

From fat quarter #6

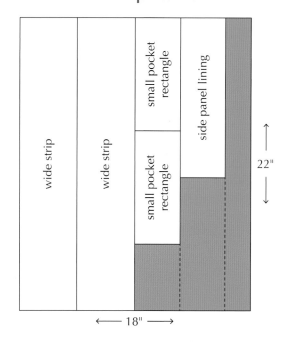

Piece	Cut	Size
wide strip	2	$4^1/_2$" wide
small pocket rectangle	2	$8^1/_2$" x $3^1/_2$"
side panel lining	1	$3^1/_2$" x 12"

From fusible fleece

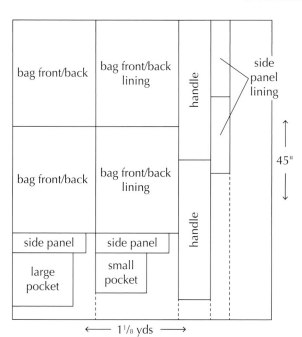

Piece	Cut	Size
bag front/back and bag front/back lining	4	16" x 13"
side panel and side panel lining	4	3" x $11^1/_2$"
large pocket	1	$9^1/_2$" x 8"
small pocket	1	8" x 6"
handle	2	5" x 21"

MAKING THE BAG FRONT AND BACK

*Follow **Piecing**, page 62, and **Pressing**, page 63, to make bag. Use ¹/₄" seam allowances throughout.*

Note: When fusing fleece to fabric, place fleece, fusible side up, on ironing board. Center fabric, right side up, on top of fleece. Iron on the fabric side; do not place hot iron directly on fusible fleece.

1. Sew 1 **medium strip** and 1 **narrow strip** together to make **Strip Set A**. Make 2 Strip Set A's. Cut across Strip Set A's at 2¹/₂" intervals to make a total of 16 **Unit 1's**.

Strip Set A (make 2)

2¹/₂"

Unit 1 (make 16)

2. Sew 2 **wide strips** of different fabrics and 1 **narrow strip** together to make **Strip Set B**. Make 3 Strip Set B's. Cut across Strip Set B's at 2¹/₂" intervals to make a total of 16 **Unit 2's**.

Strip Set B (make 3)

2¹/₂"

Unit 2 (make 16)

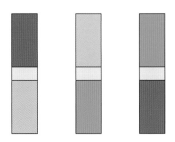

3. Sew 1 Unit 1 and 1 Unit 2 together to make **Unit 3**. Make 16 Unit 3's.

Unit 3 (make 16)

4. Placing Units in desired order and rotating every other Unit, sew 8 Unit 3's together to make **Bag Front**. Bag Front should measure 16¹/₂" x 13¹/₂" including seam allowances. Repeat to make **Bag Back**.

Bag Front/Back (make 2)

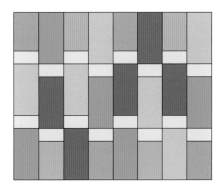

5. Fuse corresponding fleece pieces to Bag Front and Bag Back.
6. Follow **Quilting**, page 63, to quilt Bag Front and Bag Back as desired. Bag shown is quilted in the ditch along the vertical seams.

MAKING THE BAG FRONT AND BACK LINING

1. Fuse corresponding fleece pieces to **bag front/back linings**.
2. Sew 2 **large pocket rectangles** together to make **large pocket**. Make 2 large pockets.

Large Pocket (make 2)

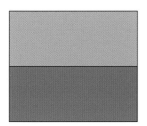

3. Sew 2 **small pocket rectangles** together to make **small pocket**. Make 2 small pockets.

Small Pocket (make 2)

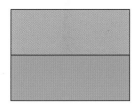

4. Fuse corresponding fleece pieces to 1 large pocket and 1 small pocket.
5. With right sides together and leaving one long edge open, sew large pockets together. Clip corners, turn, and press. Repeat with small pockets.

6. With raw edges of pocket 3¾" from bottom edge of lining, center 1 pocket horizontally on right side of bag front lining *(Fig. 1)*. Sew raw edge of pocket to bag front lining.

Fig. 1

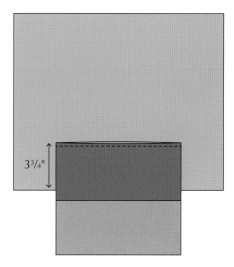

3¾"

7. Press pocket up; pin. Topstitch ¼" from side and bottom edges of pocket *(Fig. 2)*.

Fig. 2

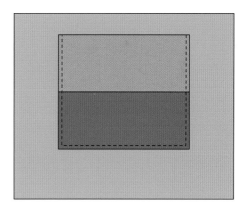

8. With raw edges of pocket 6" from bottom edge of lining, repeat Steps 6-7 to sew small pocket to bag back lining.

MAKING THE SIDE PANELS

1. Fuse corresponding fleece pieces to **side panels** and **side panel linings**.

MAKING THE HANDLES

1. Fuse corresponding fleece pieces to **handles**.
2. Matching **wrong sides** and long edges, press 1 handle in half. Open up and press long edges to meet pressed crease *(Fig. 3)*. Matching folded edges, press handle in half again. Repeat with remaining handle.

Fig. 3

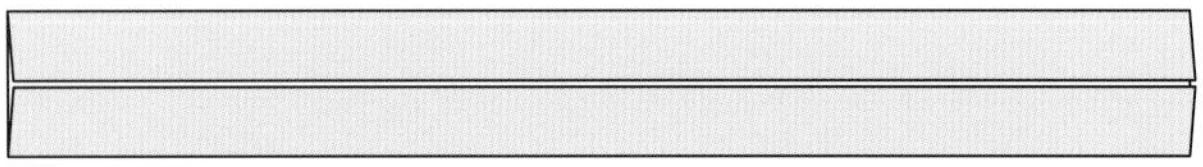

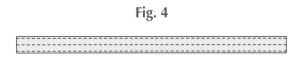

3. Topstitch approximately $1/8$" from folded edges and in center of each handle *(Fig. 4)*.

Fig. 4

4. Extending ends of handle $1/4$" beyond top of Bag Front, pin 1 handle to right side of Bag Front $3^5/8$" from Bag Front sides *(Fig. 5)*. Keeping stitches within the $1/4$" seam allowance, zigzag stitch handle ends to Bag Front; stitch back and forth 2 or 3 times. Repeat to add remaining handle to Bag Back.

Fig. 5

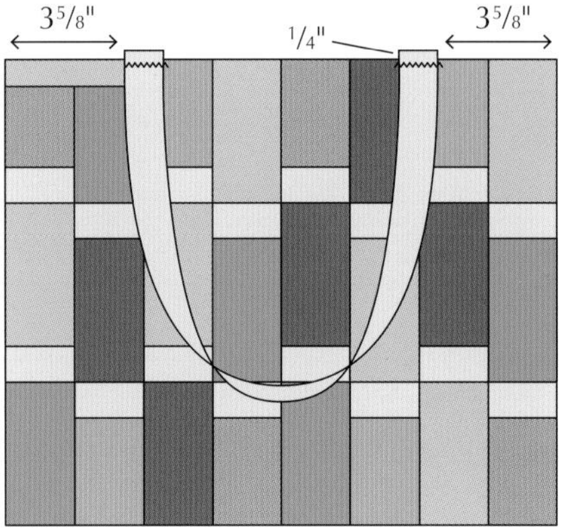

ASSEMBLING THE BAG

1. Sew Bag Front and Bag Back together along bottom edge *(Fig. 6)*.

Fig. 6

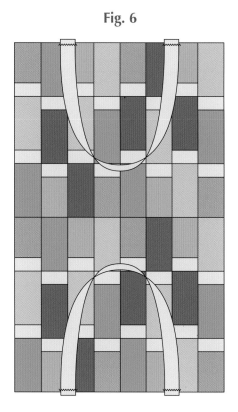

2. Aligning top edges and stopping and backstitching $1/4$" from bottom edge of side panel, sew 1 side panel to one side of Bag Front *(Fig. 7)*. Sew remaining side panel to other side of Bag Front *(Fig. 8)*.

Fig. 7

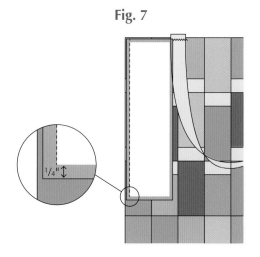

Fig. 8

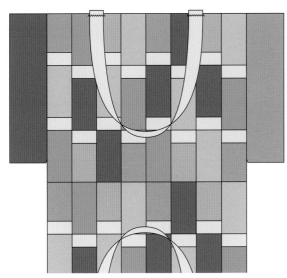

3. In the same manner, sew side panels to sides of Bag Back *(Fig. 9)*.

Fig. 9

4. Backstitching at beginning and end of stitching, sew bottom edges of side panels to Bag Front/Back *(Fig. 10)* to complete **outer bag**. Turn outer bag right side out.

Fig. 10

5. Leaving a 5" opening along bottom edge, repeat Steps 1-4 using lining pieces to make **bag lining**. Do not turn bag lining right side out.

6. Matching right sides and top edges, place outer bag inside bag lining. Sew outer bag and bag lining together along top edge. Turn bag right side out through opening in bag lining. Sew opening closed. Place bag lining inside outer bag.

7. Topstitch ¹/₄" from top edge of bag.

8. To make optional **bottom insert**, sew **insert covers** together leaving 1 short end open. Clip corners and turn right side out. Slip template plastic in cover and stitch opening closed. Place bottom insert in bottom of bag.

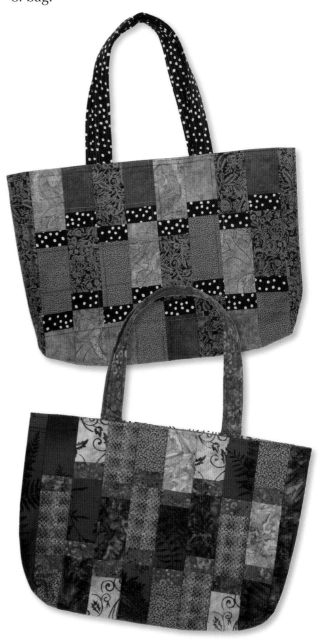

Fun black and white dots (upper bag) and a contrasting green print (lower bag) were used for the handles and narrow strips in these versions of Sausalito.

sonoma

Finished Bag Size: Approximately 15½" x 12¾" x 1½" (39 cm x 32 cm x 4 cm)

SHOPPING LIST

Fat quarters are approximately 22" x 18" (56 cm x 46 cm).

☐ 6 assorted fat quarters

☐ 1 yd (91 cm) of 45" (114 cm) wide Pellon® fusible fleece

Optional: For a more rigid bag bottom, you will also need the following to make bottom insert. (Bag shown does not have insert.)

☐ 1 piece of template plastic 15½" x 1½" (39 cm x 4 cm)

☐ 2 pieces of fabric 16⅛" x 2⅛" (41 cm x 5 cm) for **insert covers**

CUTTING THE PIECES

*Follow tables and cutting diagrams and **Rotary Cutting**, page 61, to cut fabric. All measurements include ¼" seam allowances.*

From *each* of fat quarters #1 and #2

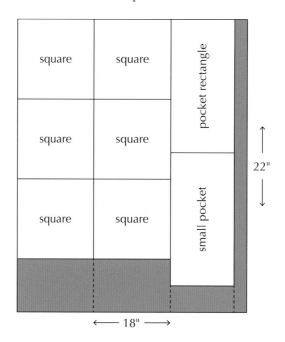

Piece	Cut	Size
square	6	6" x 6"
pocket rectangle	1	10" x 5"
small pocket	1	10" x 5"

From fat quarter #3

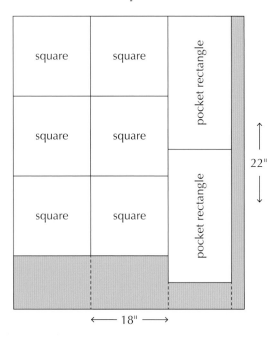

Piece	Cut	Size
square	6	6" x 6"
pocket rectangle	2	10" x 5"

From fat quarter #4

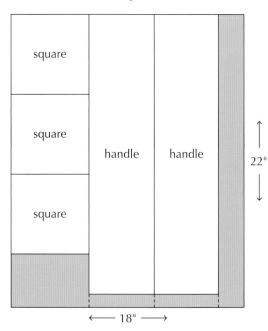

Piece	Cut	Size
square	3	6" x 6"
handle	2	5" x 21"

From *each* of fat quarters #5 and #6

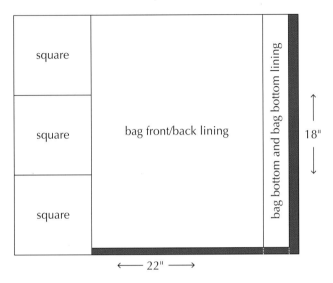

Piece	Cut	Size
square	3	6" x 6"
bag front/back lining	1	17½" x 13¼"
bag bottom and bag bottom lining	1	17½" x 2"

From fusible fleece

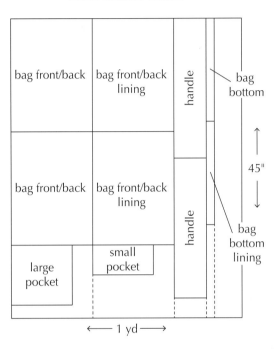

Piece	Cut	Size
bag front/back and bag front/back lining	4	17" x 12¾"
large pocket	1	9½" x 9"
small pocket	1	9½" x 4½"
handle	2	5" x 21"
bag bottom and bag bottom lining	2	17" x 1½"

MAKING THE BAG FRONT AND BACK

*Follow **Piecing**, page 62, and **Pressing**, page 63, to make bag. Use ¹/₄" seam allowances throughout.*

Note: When fusing fleece to fabric, place fleece, fusible side up, on ironing board. Center fabric, right side up, on top of fleece. Iron on the fabric side; do not place hot iron directly on fusible fleece.

1. Make 9 stacks of 3 **squares** of 3 different fabrics.
2. Place 1 stack on cutting mat. Using the blue lines in *Fig. 1* as a suggestion, rotary cut 2 gentle curves in opposite corners of squares.

Fig. 1

3. Arrange the pieces into sets that have 1 piece from each of the 3 fabrics *(Fig. 2)*. Keep the pieces of each set together with pin or zip bag.

Fig. 2

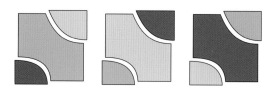

4. Repeat Steps 2-3 with each remaining stack.
5. Select 1 set of pieces. Fold each curved edge in half and finger press fold to mark center of curve.
6. With center piece on top and matching right sides and center marks, pin center piece and 1 corner piece together at center marks and each end *(Fig. 3)*. Easing as needed, pin around curve.

Fig. 3

back

7. With center piece on top, make a few stitches and then stop with needle down. Pivot the pieces, realign raw edges as needed, and make a few more stitches. Continue stitching, realigning edges, and easing in the fullness of the top fabric as you sew. Clip seam allowances and press. Sew remaining corner piece to center piece to make **Unit**. Edges may be uneven; **do not** trim at this time.

Unit

8. Repeat Steps 5-7 to make 27 Units. Discard the 3 smallest Units. Of the 24 remaining Units, determine the smallest. Trim smallest Unit to 4³/₄" x 4³/₄". If Unit is too small, trim it to the largest square possible. Trim remaining Units to same size as smallest Unit.
9. Referring to **Bag Front/Back** diagram, arrange 12 Units into 3 Rows of 4 Units.
10. Sew Units into Rows, and then sew Rows together to make **Bag Front**. Bag Front should measure 17¹/₂" x 13¹/₄". (If Bag Front measures less, see *Note* below.) Repeat to make **Bag Back**.

Bag Front/Back (make 2)

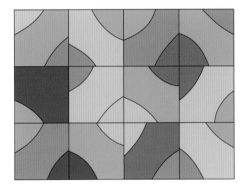

Note: If Bag Front measures less than 17¹/₂" x 13¹/₄":
• Trim **bag front/back linings** the same size as Bag Front.
• Trim fleece **bag front/backs** and **bag front/back linings** ¹/₂" smaller (width and height) than Bag Front.
• Trim **bag bottom** and **bag bottom lining** the same *width* as Bag Front.
• Trim fleece **bag bottom** and **bag bottom lining** ¹/₂" smaller (width and height) than bag bottom.

11. Fuse corresponding fleece pieces to Bag Front and Bag Back.
12. Follow **Quilting**, page 63, to quilt Bag Front and Bag Back as desired. Bag shown is machine quilted with outline quilting inside the large piece of each Unit.

MAKING THE BAG FRONT AND BACK LINING

1. Fuse corresponding fleece pieces to **bag front/back linings**.
2. Sew 2 **pocket rectangles** together along 1 long edge to make **large pocket**. Make 2 large pockets.

large pocket

3. Fuse corresponding fleece pieces to 1 large pocket and 1 **small pocket**.
4. With right sides together and leaving one long edge open, sew 2 large pockets together. Clip corners, turn, and press. Repeat with small pockets.
5. With raw edges of pocket 1¹/₄" from bottom edge of lining, center large pocket horizontally on right side of bag front lining (*Fig. 4*). Sew raw edge of pocket to bag front lining.

Fig. 4

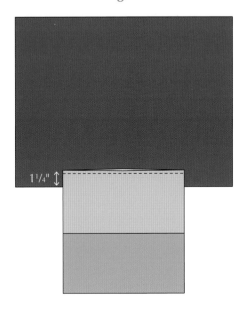

1¹/₄"

6. Press pocket up; pin. Topstitch ¼" from side and bottom edges of pocket *(Fig. 5)*.

Fig. 5

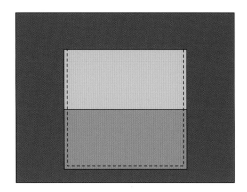

7. With raw edges of pocket 5" from bottom edge of lining, repeat Steps 5-6 to sew small pocket to bag back lining.

MAKING THE BAG BOTTOM

1. Fuse corresponding fleece pieces to **bag bottom** and **bag bottom lining**.

MAKING THE HANDLES

1. Fuse corresponding fleece pieces to **handles**.
2. Matching ***wrong sides*** and long edges, press 1 handle in half. Open up and press long edges to meet pressed crease *(Fig. 6)*. Matching folded edges, press handle in half again. Repeat with remaining handle.

Fig. 6

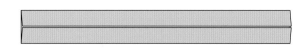

3. Topstitch approximately ⅛" from folded edges and in center of each handle *(Fig. 7)*.

Fig. 7

4. Extending ends of handle ¼" beyond top of Bag Front, pin 1 handle to right side of Bag Front 4" from Bag Front sides *(Fig. 8)*. Keeping stitches within the ¼" seam allowance of the Bag Front, zigzag stitch handle ends to Bag Front; stitch back and forth 2 or 3 times. Repeat to add remaining handle to Bag Back.

Fig. 8

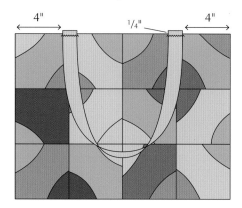

ASSEMBLING THE BAG

1. Sew Bag Front, bag bottom, and Bag Back together *(Fig. 9)*.

Fig. 9

2. Matching right sides and top edges, fold bag in half and stitch side edges to make **outer bag** *(Fig. 10)*. Do not turn outer bag right side out.

Fig. 10

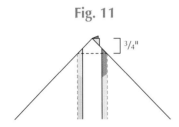

3. To form each bottom corner of bag, align 1 side seam to center of tote bottom *(Fig. 11)*. Sew across bag bottom ³/₄" from corner point. Trim seam allowances to ¹/₄". Turn outer bag right side out.

Fig. 11

4. Leaving a 5" opening along one bottom edge, repeat Steps 1-3 using lining pieces to make **bag lining**. Do not turn bag lining right side out.
5. Matching right sides and top edges, place outer bag inside bag lining. Sew outer bag and bag lining together along top edge. Turn bag right side out through opening in bag lining. Sew opening closed. Place bag lining inside outer bag.
6. Topstitch ¹/₄" from top edge of bag.
7. To make optional **bottom insert**, sew **insert covers** together leaving 1 short end open. Clip corners and turn right side out. Slip template plastic in cover and stitch opening closed. Place bottom insert in bottom of bag.

Batiks are a good choice for a Sonoma bag, like the version shown in oranges, browns, and greens. The other version includes a floral print and coordinating cream, plum, and peach prints.

general instructions

To make your quilting easier and more enjoyable, we encourage you to carefully read all of the general instructions, study the color photographs, and familiarize yourself with the individual project instructions before beginning a project.

FABRICS

SELECTING FABRICS
Choose high-quality, medium-weight 100% cotton fabric fat quarters.

PREPARING FABRICS
Pre-washing fabrics may cause edges to ravel. As a result, your fat quarters may not be large enough to cut all of the pieces required for your chosen project. Therefore, we **do not** recommend pre-washing.

Before cutting, prepare fabrics with a steam iron set on cotton and starch or sizing. The starch or sizing will give the fabric a crisp finish. This will make cutting more accurate and may make piecing easier.

ROTARY CUTTING
For best use of fat quarters, carefully follow project tables and cutting diagrams.

- Cut strips parallel to the long edge of the fabric unless otherwise indicated by cutting diagram.

- If cutting strips parallel to the long edge, place fat quarter on work surface with lengthwise (short) edge closest to you. If cutting strips parallel to the short edge, place fat quarter on work surface with crosswise (long) edge closest to you.

- Square left edge of fabric using rotary cutter and rulers *(Figs. 1-2)*.

Fig. 1

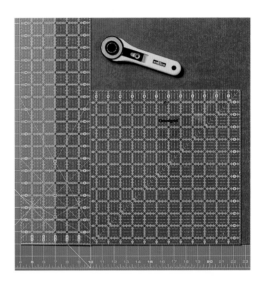

Fig. 2

- To cut each strip required for a project, place ruler over cut edge of fabric, aligning desired marking on ruler with cut edge; make cut *(Fig. 3)*.

Fig. 3

PIECING

Precise cutting, followed by accurate piecing, will ensure that all pieces of your project fit together well.

- Set sewing machine stitch length for approximately 11 stitches per inch.

- Use neutral-colored general-purpose sewing thread (not quilting thread) in needle and in bobbin.

- An accurate ¼" seam allowance is **essential**. Presser feet that are ¼" wide are available for most sewing machines.

- When piecing, always place pieces right sides together and match raw edges; pin if necessary.

- Chain piecing saves time and will usually result in more accurate piecing.

- Trim away points of seam allowances that extend beyond edges of sewn pieces.

SEWING STRIP SETS

When there are several strips to assemble into a strip set, first sew strips together into pairs, then sew pairs together to form strip set. To help avoid distortion, sew seams in opposite directions *(Fig. 4)*.

Fig. 4

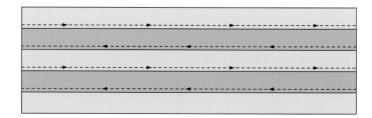

SEWING ACROSS SEAM INTERSECTIONS

When sewing across intersection of two seams, place pieces right sides together and match seams exactly, making sure seam allowances are pressed in opposite directions *(Fig. 5)*.

Fig. 5

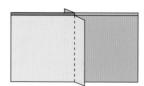

SEWING SHARP POINTS

To ensure sharp points when joining triangular or diagonal pieces, stitch across the center of the "X" (shown in pink) formed on wrong side by previous seams *(Fig. 6)*.

Fig. 6

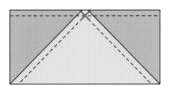

PRESSING

- Use steam iron set on "Cotton" for all pressing. ***Do not*** place hot iron directly on fusible fleece.

- Press after sewing each seam.

- Seam allowances are almost always pressed to one side, usually toward darker fabric. However, to reduce bulk it may occasionally be necessary to press seam allowances toward the lighter fabric or even to press them open.

- To prevent dark fabric seam allowance from showing through light fabric, trim darker seam allowance slightly narrower than lighter seam allowance.

QUILTING

TYPES OF QUILTING DESIGNS

In the Ditch Quilting

Quilting along seamlines is called "in the ditch" quilting. This type of quilting should be done on side **opposite** seam allowance and does not have to be marked.

Outline Quilting

Quilting a consistent distance, usually ¼", from seams is called "outline" quilting.

Channel Quilting

Quilting with straight, parallel lines is called "channel" quilting. This type of quilting may be marked or stitched using a guide.

Crosshatch Quilting

Quilting straight lines in a grid pattern is called "crosshatch" quilting. Lines may be stitched parallel to edges of quilt or stitched diagonally. This type of quilting may be marked or stitched using a guide.

Meandering Quilting

Quilting in random curved lines and swirls is called "meandering" quilting. Quilting lines should not cross or touch each other. This type of quilting does not need to be marked.

MARKING QUILTING LINES

Quilting lines may be marked using chalk pencils or removable fabric marking pens.

Caution: Pressing may permanently set some marks. **Test** different markers **on scrap fabric** to find one that marks clearly and can be thoroughly removed.

MACHINE QUILTING METHODS

Use general-purpose thread in bobbin. Do not use quilting thread. Thread the needle with general-purpose thread or transparent monofilament thread to make quilting blend with fabrics. Use decorative thread, such as a metallic or contrasting-color general-purpose thread, to make quilting lines stand out more.

Straight-Line Quilting

The term "straight-line" is somewhat deceptive, since curves (especially gentle ones) as well as straight lines can be stitched with this technique.

1. Set stitch length for six to ten stitches per inch and attach walking foot to sewing machine.
2. Determine which section will have longest continuous quilting line.
3. Begin stitching on longest quilting line, using very short stitches for the first 1/4" to "lock" quilting. Stitch across project, using one hand on each side of walking foot to slightly spread fabric and to guide fabric through machine. Lock stitches at end of quilting line.
4. Continue machine quilting, stitching longer quilting lines first before moving on to other areas.

Free-Motion Quilting

Free-motion quilting may be free form or may follow a marked pattern.

1. Attach darning foot to sewing machine and lower or cover feed dogs.
2. Position fabric/fleece layers under darning foot; lower foot. Holding top thread, take a stitch and pull bobbin thread to top of fabric/fleece layers. To "lock" beginning of quilting line, hold top and bobbin threads while making three to five stitches in place.
3. Use one hand on each side of darning foot to slightly spread fabric and to move fabric through the machine. Even stitch length is achieved by using smooth, flowing hand motion and steady machine speed. Slow machine speed and fast hand movement will create long stitches. Fast machine speed and slow hand movement will create short stitches. Move project sideways, back and forth, in a circular motion, or in a random motion to create desired designs; do not rotate project. Lock stitches at end of each quilting line.

Metric Conversion Chart

Inches x 2.54 = centimeters (cm)
Inches x 25.4 = millimeters (mm)
Inches x .0254 = meters (m)

Yards x .9144 = meters (m)
Yards x 91.44 = centimeters (cm)
Centimeters x .3937 = inches (")
Meters x 1.0936 = yards (yd)

Standard Equivalents

1/8"	3.2 mm	0.32 cm	1/8 yard	11.43 cm	0.11 m
1/4"	6.35 mm	0.635 cm	1/4 yard	22.86 cm	0.23 m
3/8"	9.5 mm	0.95 cm	3/8 yard	34.29 cm	0.34 m
1/2"	12.7 mm	1.27 cm	1/2 yard	45.72 cm	0.46 m
5/8"	15.9 mm	1.59 cm	5/8 yard	57.15 cm	0.57 m
3/4"	19.1 mm	1.91 cm	3/4 yard	68.58 cm	0.69 m
7/8"	22.2 mm	2.22 cm	7/8 yard	80 cm	0.8 m
1"	25.4 mm	2.54 cm	1 yard	91.44 cm	0.91 m